KEY IDEA 1 THERE ARE GLOBAL VARIATIONS IN ECON AND QUALITY OF LIFE

What you need to know

- Different ways of classifying parts of the world according to their level of economic development and quality of life
- Different economic and social measures of development: gross national income (GNI) per capita, birth and death rates, infant mortality, life expectancy, people per doctor, literacy rates, access to safe water, Human Development Index (HDI)
- Limitations of economic and social measures
- Link between stages of the Demographic Transition Model and the level of development
- Causes of uneven development: physical, economic and historical
- Consequences of uneven development: disparities in wealth and health, international migration

INTRODUCTION

Development refers to a change which leads to improvement. When a country develops it affects the natural world and people's lives, but different people may have different views about whether the changes are improvements, making this a complex area to study. When we look at development we often think of SEEP – social, environmental, economic and political factors.

How do we classify different parts of the world according to economic standing?

In this exam specification different countries are classified as:

- **HICs** – High-income countries (**GNI per capita of above** $12,535 in 2020)
- **NEEs** – Newly emerging economies – countries which used to rely on agriculture but have recently seen growth in their manufacturing industries and so increased income.
- **LICs** – Low-income countries (GNI per capita of less than $1,036 in 2020)

These definitions are used by the **World Bank**. However, some people criticise the use of categories like HICs and LICs as creating over-simplified divisions between 'rich' and 'poor', which can be misleading.

There are around 90 countries that fall between these two categories. For the World Bank, these are either lower-middle income or upper-middle income countries. NEEs are on their way from being a LIC to a HIC, but their path may not be straightforward. Sometimes groups of NEEs are linked together – for example the 'BRIC countries' are Brazil, Russia, India and China whilst the 'MINT countries' are Mexico, Indonesia, Nigeria and Turkey.

An alternative approach to classifying parts of the world was suggested by Hans Rosling, who used income levels and lifestyles to classify development:

- **Stage 1** – extreme poverty – the billion people living on $1-2 a day and struggling to meet the most basic needs of having water, food and shelter.
- **Stage 2** – three billion people live on $4 a day and are able to meet their basic needs, but face a lot of uncertainty.
- **Stage 3** – two billion people live on $8-$32 a day, are likely to have access to water and electricity in their homes, and face less uncertainty as they have more stable incomes.
- **Stage 4** – the billion people living on $32 or more a day are able to afford consumer goods and to travel. Their insurance, bank accounts and pensions give them a great deal of security.

It is important to realise that development happens along a **continuum** – countries change over time and don't suddenly 'hop' from being a LIC to a HIC.

Different economic and social measures of development

Economic measures of development focus on money, jobs and the economy. **Social** measures of development focus on people's living standards and quality of life.

Measures of development include:

- **Gross national income (GNI) per capita** – this takes the income of the whole country and divides it by the number of people. The income of a country includes the value of goods and services produced.
- **Birth and death rates** – the number of births/deaths per thousand people per year
- **Infant mortality** – the number of children who die under 1 year old per 1000 live births per year
- **Life expectancy** – the average number of years a person is expected to live
- **People per doctor** – the number of people in a place divided by the number of doctors
- **Literacy rates** – the percentage of people who can read and write
- **Access to safe water** – the percentage of people who are able to get hold of water which is safe to drink

Across LICs access to safe water hinders development

Human Development Index (HDI)

The Human Development Index (HDI) is a composite measure – this means it takes a range of social and economic measures and combines them into one. It incorporates:

- Life expectancy at birth
- Number of years of education
- GNI per capita

The highest HDI possible is 1 and the lowest is 0. The UK had a HDI of 0.932 in 2020 and was ranked 13th in the world (the same position as Singapore). The countries with the highest HDI were Norway, Ireland and Sweden, whilst the countries with the lowest HDI were Niger, Central African Republic and Chad.

Limitations of economic and social measures

Measures of development need to be used carefully or they can lead to misconceptions. For example, the GNI of a country may be high, but that doesn't mean that everyone will be well off. The wealth could be concentrated in urban areas rather than the countryside, in one part of the country or amongst one group of people.

It is also important to use up-to-date data as countries change over time. Data may not be available for some places and is not always accurate. Some governments are corrupt and try to influence measures of development to make their countries look better.

Calculations of GNI only take the products of the formal economy into account, but in many countries much of the economy is informal and many of the farmers produce food for their own families rather than to sell.

It can be argued that a focus on economic growth isn't necessarily a good thing. People in HICs buy large amounts of consumer goods, which can be seen as a wasteful way to use resources. Industrial development in NEEs can also lead to environmental problems such as air pollution.

tutor2u

AQA GCSE (9-1) GEOGRAPHY

PAPER 2
CHANGING ECONOMIC WORLD
STUDY BOOK

Student Name:

ABOUT THIS BOOK

The **Changing Economic World Study Book** aims to meet teacher and student needs by compiling fundamental concepts, key terminology and specified case study information for this AQA GCSE Geography Paper 2 topic. The book includes the essential content to meet the specification's requirements and enable students to secure a strong foundation in their geographical knowledge and understanding of key ideas and associated case studies / examples. Students aiming for the top grades should supplement this core knowledge through their own, independent research into case studies, to ensure their answers are unique and fully developed.

The Changing Economic World Study Book also includes a range of different styles of question for each key idea within the Changing Economic World topic, to develop exam skills. Suggested model answers and mark scheme tips are provided via the QR code on the back cover of this Study Book.

CONTENTS

Link between the stages of the Demographic Transition Model and the level of development

The Demographic Transition Model

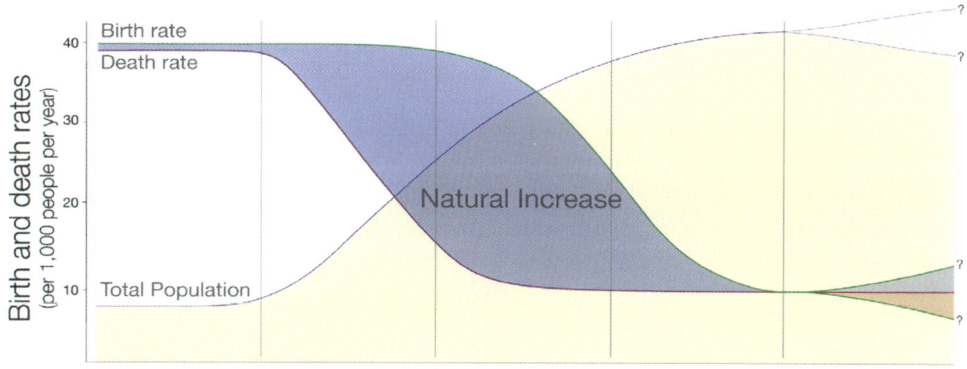

	Stage 1	Stage 2	Stage 3	Stage 4	Stage 5
Birth rate	High	High	Falling	Low	Yet to be seen (Possibly falling further, possibly rising again)
Death rate	High	Falls rapidly	Falls more slowly	Low	Low
Natural increase	Stable or slow increase	Rapid increase	Increase slows down	Falling and then stable	Little change

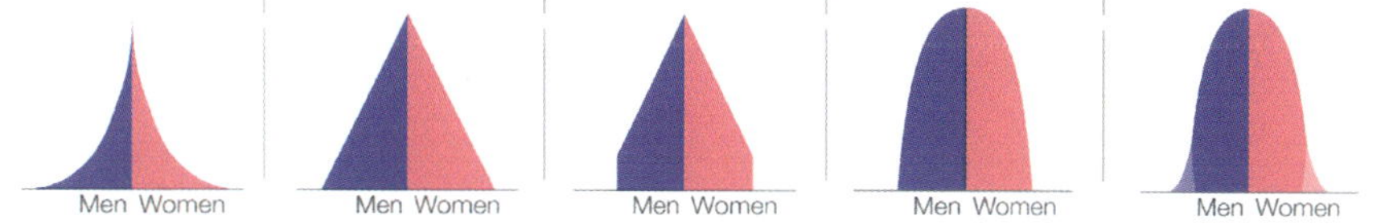

Source: https://en.wikipedia.org/wiki/Demographic_transition

The **Demographic Transition Model** (DTM) shows how the population of a place changes over time. It includes the birth rate and death rate and the difference between these – the **natural increase**. The DTM doesn't show changes in population due to migration.

This model can be used to study how a country's population changes as the country develops. Population characteristics can be shown using **population pyramids** – often know as age–sex pyramids, they show the proportion of people in different age groups. The diagram above combines the DTM and the population pyramids for each stage.

Countries face different issues in the different stages of the DTM:

- **Stage 1** – High birth and death rates, stable population – **youthful population** – people have a low life expectancy e.g. tribal communities
- **Stage 2** – High birth rate, decreasing death rate, rapid natural increase – youthful population – high demand for schools and healthcare for children e.g. Afghanistan
- **Stage 3** – Decreasing birth rate, low death rate, rapid natural increase – youthful population – high demand for schools and healthcare for children e.g. Kenya
- **Stage 4** – Low birth rate, low death rate, stable population – **ageing population** – high demand for medical and social care for the elderly e.g. France

Life expectancy is high in Japan due to the focus on a good diet and plenty of exercise

- **Stage 5** – Very low birth rate, low death rate, natural decrease – ageing population – shortage of workers, very high demand for care for the elderly e.g. Japan

The DTM can be criticised because it was produced by looking at the development of countries such as the UK and USA. Other countries may not develop in the same way.

Causes of uneven development

Places develop at different rates and may experience setbacks. This leads to uneven development across the world. Many of the causes of uneven development are interrelated.

Physical causes

- **Landlocked countries** – if a country doesn't have a coastline it is more difficult to trade. Uganda is an example of a landlocked country, many of its exports are shipped across Lake Victoria to Kenya and then taken by train to the ocean port at Mombasa.
- **Drainage networks** – countries with long rivers which are navigable (can be used by ships) can transport goods and people more easily than countries with shorter rivers or rivers which are difficult to navigate due to rapids or shallow sections. The River Mississippi in the USA drains a third of the country and has been a major factor in the development of farming and industry.
- **Temperature** – tropical diseases such as sleeping sickness and malaria have a devastating impact on the health of people and livestock. Sick people will be less productive than healthy people. Cold winters in countries such as the UK kill off pests which can affect crops, but these pests thrive in the warm tropics.
- **Rainfall** – if a place has too little or unreliable rainfall people may not have safe water to drink or enough water for farming and industry. The Sahel region of Africa often suffers from droughts, limiting its development.
- **Natural hazards** – different parts of the world are prone to droughts, floods, tropical storms or earthquakes, which can lead to water shortages, crop failure and destruction of buildings and infrastructure. Typhoon Haiyan killed 6300 people in the Philippines in 2013 and destroyed 90% of the city of Tacloban. The typhoon led to flooding and landslides, which blocked roads, and shortages of clean water led to the spread of disease.

Drought and desertification causes issues for farming and industry

Economic causes

- **Trade** – countries can become wealthier by trading with others, but different countries have different goods and services to sell, leading to differences in wealth. Many LICs export raw materials which don't sell for as a high price as processed goods; and see great changes in price in short periods of time, leading to instability. An example is Zambia, which mainly exports copper. When people started using plastic for pipes rather than copper the price of copper crashed, which was devastating for Zambia. NEEs have developed their manufacturing industries as part of their development.
- **Trade blocs** – countries may join together to form trade blocs which have free trade between member countries and charge taxes for non-member countries to trade with them. An example of a trade bloc is the European Union.
- **TNCs – Transnational corporations** have offices and factories in several countries and can move around the world to find the cheapest workers and raw materials. This means they can produce their goods and services cheaply, making it hard for smaller businesses to compete.
- **Debt** – countries may borrow money from organisations such as the World Bank. Zambia, like many LICs, did this in the 1970s so that they could develop their copper industry, but then prices for copper crashed and interest rates shot up, leaving Zambia with a debt of nearly US$7 million at the end of the 1980s.

Historical causes

- **Colonialism** – the Berlin Conference of 1884-1885 divided Africa into colonies ruled by fourteen European nations. This conference didn't involve any African rulers and didn't consider ethnic or language groups when decisions on boundaries were made. Resistance was met with force. Natural resources were exploited and the wealth sent to Europe. In possibly the worst example of exploitation, King Leopold II of Belgium became the sole owner of the Congo Free State and forced local people to collect ivory from elephants and rubber from trees in the rainforest to boost his personal wealth. The Congolese people were treated terribly and around 10 million may have died as a result. However, infrastructure such as railway lines built by imperial powers was useful for local people as well as for exploiting resources and so supported development.

- **Trade routes** – as explorers made connections between different places in the past, trade routes developed. The Silk Road connected South-east Asia and East Asia with Persia, East Africa and Southern Europe. It became famous for the trade of silk from China, but was used for many goods, helping areas along the route to develop.
- **Slavery** – between 12-15 million people were transported from Africa to the Caribbean and North America to be slaves between the 1600s and 1800s. Slavery had happened before, but not on this scale or as part of an industrialised system. The money from the sale of slaves and from the trade in goods produced using their labour (tobacco & sugar), mainly went to Europeans. In the UK many of the great buildings and institutions from the past have links to the slave trade.
- **Independence** – after World War II the European powers found themselves struggling to manage their own countries and their colonies. From 1950 onwards many colonies gained independence. Some countries have developed rapidly since independence. When Botswana became independent from Britain in 1966 it was one of the poorest countries in the world, but a good government used the wealth from the diamond mines to develop the country. The GNI per capita in Botswana has risen from $100 in 1966 to $7600 in 2018. Other countries have struggled since independence, including the Democratic Republic of Congo (DRC), which became independent from Belgium in 1960. Like Botswana, the DRC has vast reserves of precious raw materials, but in the DRC this has led to conflict. The Congolese also suffer from diseases including cholera, hepatitis A, malaria, measles and typhoid. Life expectancy in the DRC is only 48 years, whereas life expectancy in Botswana is 69 years.
- **Conflict** – whether conflict is between just two tribes or involves a massive invasion, it will cause death and destruction, limiting development in a place.

Consequences of uneven development

Differences in development between places lead to disparities in wealth and health. They also mean that some people want to leave less developed countries to move to more developed parts of the world.

Disparities in wealth

- Qatar is the wealthiest country in the world (GNI per capita of $116 799 in 2020).
- The USA was the **fastest growing economy** in 2019 due to the success of its service industries and its transnational corporations (TNCs).
- It is hard to know which is the poorest country in the world as it is difficult to get accurate data, but Central African Republic has a GNI per capita of only $663.
- Some countries had shrinking economies in 2019, such as Venezuela, Iran and Zimbabwe.

Disparities in health

- Wealthier countries have more money to **invest** in healthcare and people can afford to have **healthy lifestyles**. However, whilst the USA has the highest investment in healthcare per head, the life expectancy is shorter and people experience more injuries and illnesses than people in many other HICs.
- Far fewer people die of **infectious diseases** and more die of **chronic diseases** such as heart disease, cancer and dementia in wealthy countries due to ageing populations.
- Less wealthy countries have less infrastructure to support healthcare and less money to invest, whilst people may have poor diets. However, whilst Cuba's GNI per capita of $7,480 is well below that of a HIC, it has one of the best healthcare systems in the world because the government has focussed its spending on health.
- Infectious diseases such as HIV/AIDS, diarrhoea, malaria and TB cause many more deaths in less wealthy countries than in wealthy countries.

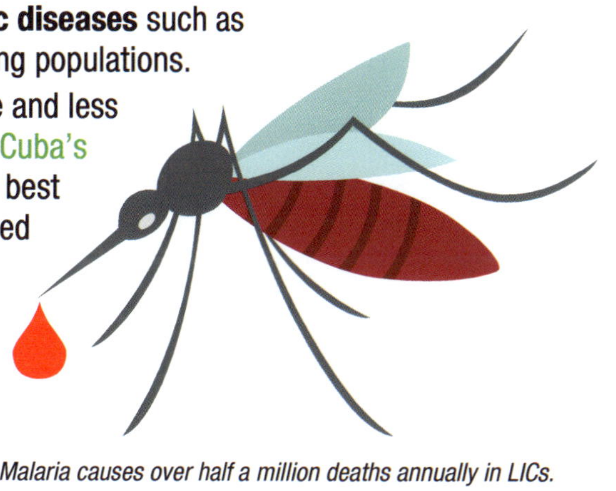

Malaria causes over half a million deaths annually in LICs.

International migration

Every day hundreds of migrants make the dangerous journey across the Mediterranean Sea to

- Migration is the movement of people from place to place. Uneven development can lead to **international Imigration** as people move from less developed countries to countries with higher levels of development.
- Different waves of migration have happened in the UK in the past. The British Nationality Act 1948 gave people living in British colonies citizen status and the right to move to the UK to live. The government encouraged people from the Caribbean to come to the UK to live and work, to fill labour shortages after WWII. Between 1948 and 1970 nearly half a million people made this journey, becoming known as the 'Windrush generation'.
- However, in 2012 the 'hostile environment' migration policy was introduced in the UK, making it difficult for people to stay in the UK without 'leave to remain' and making new migrants less welcome. As the Windrush generation hadn't been given official paperwork to say they were British citizens, many found themselves being treated as illegal immigrants and facing possible deportation.
- Europe has also faced migration issues, with over 1 million refugees from Syria, Afghanistan and Iraq crossing the Mediterranean Sea between January 2015 and March 2016. All three of these countries have suffered conflict which has affected their level of development. In April 2015 an estimated 1,200 refugees died when their boats sank whilst attempting this journey.

Question 1 | Match the terms with their definitions.

A	A country with a GNI per capita greater than $12,535GNI per head of $12 536 or above	
B	A country which has developed rapidly in recent years	
C	A country with a GNI per capita of less than $1,036 GNI per head of $1 035 or below	
D	A change that leads to improvement	

Development	NEE	HIC	LIC

Question 2 | Are these statements true or false?

All countries are either HICs or LICs.	
Gross national income (GNI) calculations include the formal economy but not the informal economy.	
Around 1 billion people live in extreme poverty in the world.	
The population of a country is a useful measure of the development of the country.	
The number of people per doctor in a country is a useful measure of the development of a country.	

The Human Development Index includes life expectancy, number of years in education and GNI per capita.	
The UK had the highest HDI score in the world in 2019.	
Stage 3 of the DTM has a decreasing birth rate, a low death rate and rapid natural increase, leading to a youthful population.	
Japan is at stage 5 of the DTM because it has natural decrease and an ageing population.	
A landlocked country has no coastline, which limits trade and so development.	
Development in the UK has been limited by cold winters which kill off pests which could eat crops.	
Trade blocs make it easier for countries outside the bloc to export goods to countries who are members of the bloc.	
In the 1970s many LICs took loans from the World Bank which left them in debt.	
The Silk Road led to the development of places along its route in the past.	
European countries benefited from wealth created as a result of slavery between the 1600s and the 1800s.	
The Berlin Conference included African and European leaders who worked together to divide Africa into colonies, using existing ethnic and language divisions to decide on boundaries.	
Botswana has developed rapidly since independence in 1966.	
The DRC has developed rapidly since independence in 1960.	
The USA invests most money in healthcare and has the best healthcare system in the world.	
People in HICs are more likely to die of chronic diseases such as heart disease and cancer rather than infectious diseases.	
People in the British colonies were given British citizenship and encouraged to move to the UK to work following the 1948 British Nationality Act.	
The 'hostile environment' policy of 2012 was introduced to make sure people who were hostile to migrants in the UK were punished.	
Around a million people from Syria, Afghanistan and Iraq crossed the Mediterranean Sea between Jan 2015 and March 2016 to escape from war and poverty and make new lives in Europe.	

Question 3 | What do these acronyms stand for?

Acronym	
HIC	*High income country*
LIC	
NEE	
GNI per capita	
HDI	
DTM	
TNC	

Question 4 | What is the difference between…

… death rate and infant mortality?	
… stage 2 of the DTM and stage 4 of the DTM?	
… an ageing population and a youthful population?	
… a country that is landlocked and one that isn't?	
… a colony and an independent country?	

Question 5 | Draw sketches of population pyramids for each stage of the DTM.

Stage 1	Stage 2	Stage 3
	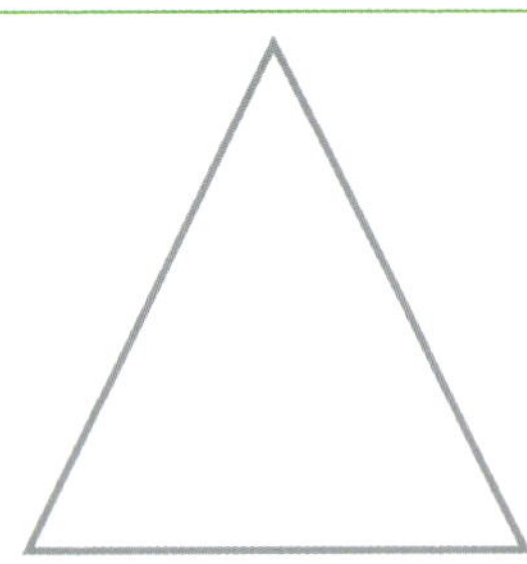	

Stage 4	Stage 5

Question 6 | Sort the statements to show if they are physical, economic or historical causes of uneven development.

- TNCs are global and so can produce goods and services cheaply, making them hard to compete with.
- Trade routes such as the Silk Road helped countries along their route to develop.
- Landlocked countries find it harder to trade.
- Countries can become wealthier by trading with each other.
- Long navigable rivers help countries develop.
- 14 European countries ruled colonies in Africa following the Berlin Conference and gained wealth from exploiting natural resources.
- Tropical diseases and pests can limit development.
- Slavery helped some European countries to become wealthy.
- Trade blocs help member countries trade with each other.
- Countries may borrow money and get into debt.
- Unreliable or too little rainfall causes shortages of water for drinking, farming and industry.
- The Congo Free State suffered terribly under the rule of Leopold II of Belgium.
- Past conflicts have held development back in places.
- Weather hazards which affect development include droughts, floods and tropical storms.
- Botswana has developed rapidly since becoming independent from Britain in 1966

Physical causes	Economic causes	Historical causes

Question 7 | Fill the gaps using the words below.

Measures of development need to be used carefully or they can lead to ____________________. For example, the GNI of a country may be high, but that doesn't mean that everyone will be well off. The wealth could be concentrated in the ____________ areas rather than the countryside, in one part of the country, or with one group of people.

It is also important to use ________________________ as countries change over time. Data may not be available for some places and is not always accurate. Some governments are ________________ and try to influence measures of development to make their countries look better.

Calculations of GNI only take the products of the _______________ into account, but in many countries much of the economy is _________________ and many of the farmers produce food for their own families rather than to sell.

It can be argued that a focus on economic growth isn't necessarily a good thing. People in HICs buy large amounts of ____________________, which can be seen as a wasteful way to use resources. Industrial development in NEEs can also lead to ________________________________ such as air pollution.

urban	corrupt	misconceptions	up-to-date data
formal economy	environmental problems	consumer goods	informal

Question 8 | To what extent do you agree with these statements? Give at least one reason why.

It is useful to categorise countries as HICs, LICs and NEEs.

I strongly/somewhat/don't agree because…

GNI per capita is a useful measure of development.

I strongly/somewhat/don't agree because…

Colonies in Africa benefitted from being ruled by European countries.

I strongly/somewhat/don't agree because…

Question 9 | Match the statements with the examples.

A landlocked country	The Philippines
An area which suffers from droughts	European Union
The country hit by Typhoon Haiyan in 2013	Belgium
An example of a trade bloc	Botswana
Country ruled by King Leopold II who owned the Congo Free State	The Sahel
A country which has developed rapidly since independence	Uganda

Question 10 | Exam-style question.

Assess the causes of uneven development across the world.
(6 marks)

KEY IDEA 2 VARIOUS STRATEGIES EXIST FOR REDUCING THE GLOBAL DEVELOPMENT GAP

What you need to know

An overview of the strategies used to reduce the development gap: investment, industrial development and tourism, aid, using use of intermediate technology, fairtrade, debt relief, microfinance loans

An example of how the growth of tourism in an LIC or NEE helps to reduce the development gap

INTRODUCTION

Whilst countries across the globe range in development across a continuum, the gap between the most developed and least developed countries is still significant. Organisations such as the United Nations (UN), national governments and non-governmental organisations (NGOs) are developing strategies with the aim of closing this gap.

Strategies to reduce the development gap

Investment and industrial development

One cause of uneven development is differences in trade between low-income and high-income countries. Many LICs trade raw materials, which have low and rapidly changing prices. Investing money in developing **manufacturing industries** can help countries to develop economically, closing the development gap.

China is investing $900 billion in its Belt and Road initiative which aims to develop **infrastructure** to connect East Africa, Europe and Asia, creating a modern Silk Road trade route. China became Africa's most important trading partner in 2009 and more than a million Chinese workers have moved to Africa.

Investment can bring a **multiplier effect**, where one event triggers another. If a **transnational corporation** (TNC) builds a factory in a town it will provide jobs, meaning people will have more money to spend in local shops. It may also buy raw materials from local businesses and sell its products in local shops. This all helps to generate money within the local economy, and can encourage future investment.

However, investment and development projects may benefit the investors more than the **host country**. Some people are concerned about the power China will have in areas which have received investment. TNCs return profits to their home countries rather than staying within the host country.

Aid

Aid means help and may take many different forms - money, goods, technology and expertise. **Bilateral aid** (from one government to another) may come with many conditions attached to make sure the aid is used in a particular way and sometimes to ensure both countries benefit. **Multilateral aid** (from organisations such as the World Bank) may also have conditions attached. Aid from **NGOs** tends to be smaller scale, but often comes with fewer conditions.

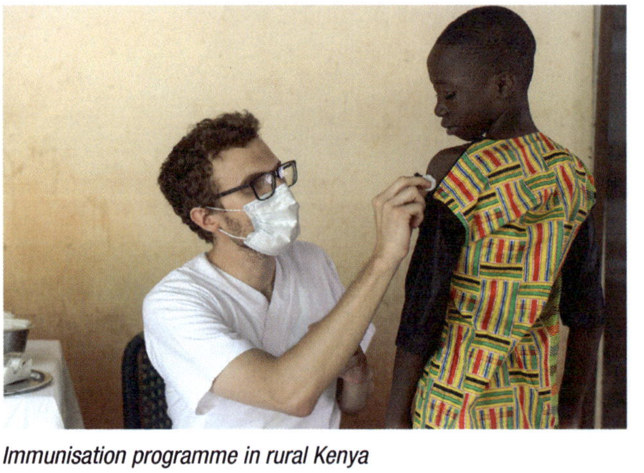

Immunisation programme in rural Kenya

Some countries have committed to a UN target of spending 0.7% of their GNI on overseas aid. The UK spent one third of its aid budget on multilateral aid in 2016, with the rest spent on bilateral aid. Most of this bilateral aid was spent on Pakistan, Syria, Ethiopia, Nigeria and Afghanistan. Approximately 15% of overseas aid from the UK was spent on **short term aid** projects. The remaining 85% was spent on **long term developmental aid** including vaccination programmes, education and healthcare. Some aid spending has been criticised as being wasteful or going to countries that are corrupt or could afford to support their own development initiatives.

Local small-scale aid projects are focused on a small area and can make a big difference in the areas they support. Excellent is an NGO which pioneered the use of sand dams in Kenya to tackle desertification. They work with local people to decide where to build dams across ephemeral rivers (rivers that only flow for part of the year). These dams silt up in a couple of years, then when rain falls it is stored in the sand behind the dam, protected from evaporation and contamination. The rain water that would have lasted a few weeks will last for several months.

Aid projects can reduce the development gap by improving healthcare, education and water and food security, meaning that people are healthier and more educated, making them and their country more productive.

Intermediate technology

This is a type of **appropriate technology** which focuses on technology which is more efficient than the technology it replaces but still doesn't cost much. It takes a **sustainable** approach, benefitting the environment and local people, and ensures that local people are part of the decision-making process.

Sand dams are an example of **intermediate technology**. The NGO supports the community in building the stone and concrete dams, water tanks and hand pumps. The dams need very little maintenance and last for 60 years or more. This technology reduces the development gap by tackling problems of **food and water insecurity**, improving people's quality of life.

Fair trade

Products sold with the Fairtrade logo on them show a commitment to better prices, working conditions and terms of trade for farmers and workers, and in return, farmers agree to farm using sustainable techniques. Sales of Fairtrade products contribute to a **Fairtrade Premium** to be spent on community projects. Ben and Jerry's ice cream is made using vanilla from Fairtrade farmers in Madagascar and Uganda. More than $278,000 was raised in Fairtrade premiums in 2018 and was used to improve a health centre, repair a school and build an office.

Fairtrade coffee farmer in the Mount Elgon region of Uganda

Some criticisms have been made of Fairtrade. Only richer consumers can afford the extra cost of Fairtrade products and some organisations have created their own form of Fairtrade labelling which doesn't guarantee the same benefits as the official Fairtrade scheme.

Fairtrade reduces the development gap by improving pay, meaning that farmers and workers can improve their homes and send their children to school. The Fairtrade premium improves health care and education, providing healthy and skilled workers for the future.

Debt relief

Many LICs borrowed money from the World Bank in the 1970s to develop their countries, but when interest rates rose sharply in the 1980s their debts spiralled out of control, leading to a **debt crisis**. Zambia borrowed money to develop its copper industry, but then prices for copper crashed and interest rates shot up, leaving Zambia with a debt of nearly $7 million at the end of the 1980s.

In 2005, the group of eight of the world's richest and most powerful countries, known as the G8, voted to cancel many of the debts of heavily indebted poor countries (HIPCs) as long as they showed they could manage their finances, weren't corrupt and would spend the money they saved on poverty reduction. By 2015, 36 countries had their debts to the International Monetary Fund (IMF) cancelled, saving them $75 million, but debts to other organisations remained. Some countries have taken out additional loans since receiving debt relief.

Debt relief has meant that money that would have been spent on debt can be spent on education, health care and poverty reduction, helping to close the development gap.

Microfinance

Banks, such as the Grameen Bank in Bangladesh, have been set up to loan small amounts of money to people so that they can improve their lives. These **microfinance** loans are used to start or improve small businesses. The borrowers are often people who don't have access to traditional banks. They pay back the loan with a small amount of interest and can use the profits they make to improve their homes, send their children to school and pay for healthcare, helping to close the development gap.

Tourism

Uganda: An example of how the growth of tourism in an LIC helps to reduce the development gap.

Uganda is a country with great potential for tourism which is not yet being fully realised. The ten national parks are the country's main attraction, with Uganda and neighbouring Rwanda the only places tourists can see mountain gorillas in their natural habitat. Tourists also visit the source of the Nile at Lake Victoria and Uganda's capital city, Kampala.

The World Travel and Tourism Council report of 2018 shows that tourism contributed almost $1,914 million to Uganda's GNI in 2017, 7.3% of its total GNI. Over 600,000 jobs have been created in the tourism industry, 6.3% of total employment. Both figures were expected to rise in 2018.

Tourism spending in Uganda leads to a **multiplier effect**. It costs $40 for a tourist to enter Murchinson Falls National Park for a day visit. This money is used to pay the wages of the gate staff and rangers in the park and to carry out work to conserve its environment.

However, there is **conflict** over how the park's resources should be used. An application from the energy company Total E&P Uganda to develop six oilfields in the park has been approved by the government and a feasibility study is being carried out to help decided if a hydro-electricity plant should be built at Uhuru Falls (next to Murchinson Falls). Chinese **investment** is supporting these plans and the road network has already been improved. Exploiting these resources could help Uganda to close the development gap more rapidly, but at a cost to the natural environment and local people.

Seeing giraffes in the wild draws tourists to Murchinson Falls National Park

Climate Action Uganda have asked the government to invest in biogas and solar power instead. They point out that tourism is Uganda's leading export earner and that around a third of tourists make Murchinson National Park part of their visit to Uganda, with a multiplier effect for drivers, hoteliers and craft makers. They see the growth of tourism as vital in closing the development gap in a sustainable way.

However, tourism not a reliable way to reduce the development as is hit hard in times of recession and ceased entirely during the coronavirus crisis of 2020, leaving tourist areas with little income.

Question 1 | Match the terms with their definitions

	Definition	Answer
A	Buying and selling goods between countries	trade
B	The difference between the wealth and well-being of LICs and HICs	development gap
C	Helping others	aid
D	Progress of a country considering wealth and & well-being	development

Development gap	Trade	Development	Aid

Question 2 | Are these statements true or false?

All countries have an equal opportunity to increase their wealth through trade	false
Developing manufacturing and processing industries can help countries develop economically	true
Chinese organisations are investing in infrastructure, industry and tourism across the world	true
A multiplier effect means that the people in charge of an organisation see their investments multiplied	true
Multilateral aid is aid from one country to another	true
The UK spends 0.7% of its GNI on overseas aid	true
Most overseas aid from the UK is short term aid in emergency situations	false
Intermediate technology is a type of appropriate technology which is more efficient than the technology it replaces but is still low cost	true
The only difference between Fairtrade and non-Fairtrade products is the amount of money paid to the farmers	False
Many LICs borrowed money to develop their countries in the 1970s but their debts spiralled out of control in the 1980s, holding development back	true
The agreement to give HIPCs debt relief meant that all of their debts were wiped out	False
Debt relief helps to close the development gap because countries can spend their money on improving education and healthcare instead of using it to pay back debts	true
Microfinance loans are small loans made available to people who often can't use traditional banks so that they can invest in their own small businesses	true
Everyone agrees that the priority in Murchinson Falls National Park in Uganda should be to welcome tourists and that industrial development should be avoided	False
Tourism is Uganda's leading export earner	true

Question 3 | What do these acronyms stand for?	
Acronym	
HIC	***High income country***
LIC	low income country
NEE	Newly emerging economy
TNC	Trans National Corporation
NGO	non governmental organisation
HIPC	heavily indebtedted poor countries (38)
IMF	international monetuary fund
G8	group of eight of the world's richest and most powerful countries (UK, paris, germany, italy, japan, USA, canada and russia

Question 4 | How could the development gap close if…	
… women who haven't been able to use banks before can apply for microfinance loans?	
… Chinese investment is used to build a new railway connection from a landlocked country to an ocean port?	
… the World Bank provides multilateral aid to the government of a LIC?	
… a sand dam is built across an ephemeral river in a dry part of Kenya?	
… a farmer in Madagascar sells their vanilla to be used in Ben and Jerry's ice cream as part of the Fairtrade scheme?	
… a HIPC has its debt to the IMF cancelled?	

Question 5 | Draw a diagram to show how investment can lead to a multiplier effect in a place

Question 6 | Fill the gaps using the words below

Many LICs borrowed money from the World Bank in the 1970s to develop their countries, but when interest rates rose sharply in the 1980s their debts spiralled out of control, leading to a debt crisis. Zambia borrowed money to develop the copper industry, but then prices for copper crashed and interest rates shot up, leaving Zambia with a debt of nearly $7 million at the end of the 1980s.

In 2005 the group of eight of the world's richest and most powerful countries known as the G8 voted to cancel many of the debts of heavily indebted poor countries (HIPCs) as long as they showed they could manage their finances, weren't corrupt and would spend the money they saved on poverty reduction. By 2015, 36 countries had their debts to the International Monetary Fund (IMF) cancelled, saving them $75 million, but debts to other organisations remained. Some countries have taken out additional loans since debt relief.

Debt relief has meant that money that would have been spent on debt can be spent on education, health care and poverty reduction, helping close the development gap.

relief	indebted	develop	G8
debt crisis	poverty	gap	

Question 7 | **Complete the 'washing line of relative importance' to show how important industrial development, aid and debt relief are in reducing the development gap. Write a statement to support your choices.**

Question 8 | 'Tourism is the best way to boost development in Uganda'. Colour the thermometer to show how strongly you agree with this statement. Write a statement to support your choice. The best statements will refer to specific details related to Uganda.

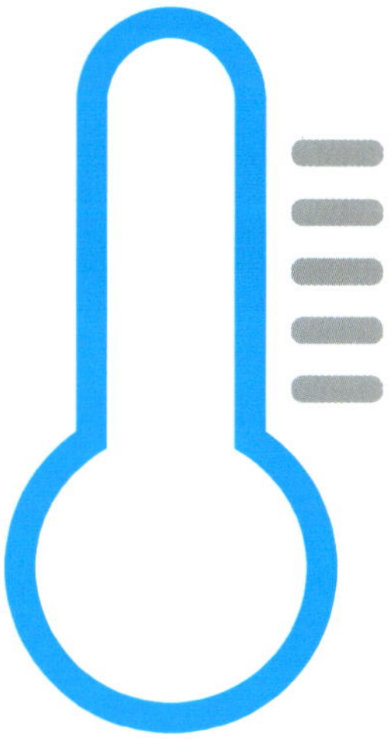

Strongly agree

Somewhat agree

Strongly disagree

Question 9 | Match the descriptions of strategies used to reduce the development gap with the examples

Descriptions	Examples
Investment in infrastructure to create a new Silk Road	Sand dams in Kenya
Intermediate technology used to improve water and food security	Debt relief following the meeting of the G8 in 2005
Paying a fair amount to farmers and generating a community premium	Chinese Belt and Road Project
Cancelling money owed to the IMF by some HIPCs	Fairtrade vanilla farming in Madagascar

Question 10 | Exam-style question.

Evaluate the effectiveness of strategies to reduce the development gap.
(9 marks)

KEY IDEA 3 SOME LICS AND NEES ARE EXPERIENCING RAPID ECONOMIC DEVELOPMENT WHICH LEADS TO SIGNIFICANT SOCIAL, ENVIRONMENTAL AND CULTURAL CHANGE

What you need to know: A case study of one LIC or NEE to illustrate
The location and importance of the country, regionally and globally
The wider political, social, cultural and environmental context within which the country is placed
The changing industrial structure. The balance between different sectors of the economy. How manufacturing industry can stimulate economic development
The role of transnational corporations (TNCs) in relation to industrial development. Advantages and disadvantages of TNC(s) to the host country
The changing political and trading relationships with the wider world
International aid: types of aid, impacts of aid on the receiving country
The environmental impacts of economic development
The effects of economic development on quality of life for the population

This Study Book includes a summary of the Nigeria case study. To see this case study in detail, scan the QR code below. You'll need to be logged into your free mytutor2u account to access this resource.

INTRODUCTION

Nigeria is a newly emerging economy (NEE) in West Africa with a GNI per head of $5,040. It has a population of around 200 million people, making it the 7th most populated country in the world.

The location and regional and global importance of Nigeria

Nigeria is **located** in West Africa and has an Atlantic coastline in the south. It is bordered by Niger, Chad, Cameroon and Benin. The capital city of Nigeria is Abuja.

Nigeria took a leading role in the creation of the African Union, promoting collaboration between nations. Nigeria has also played a peace-keeping role in West Africa.

Nigeria is important globally because of its **diaspora**. The Nigerian diaspora is the 1.24 million Nigerians living abroad in different countries, spreading Nigerian influence and culture around the world. Nigeria also plays an important part in world **trade**.

Nigeria's political, social, cultural and environmental context

Nigeria was created following the Berlin Conference in 1884 when representatives of 14 European countries divided Africa up between them. The new country of Nigeria was a **British colony**. Nigeria became independent from the British Empire in 1960.

Britain benefitted economically from its links with Nigeria. Between 1,000 – 2,000 slaves a year were purchased from Lagos by British slave traders between 1790-1807. When the Slave Trade Act made it illegal for British people to own slaves the Portuguese took over the trade in slaves from Lagos. From 1815 to 1840 the British developed a trade in palm oil from Nigeria, meaning many farmers near the coast started growing cash crops. The **infrastructure** built under British power helped Nigeria to develop, but Black Africans were sometimes used as forced labour in projects such as building railway lines.

Nigeria's first democracy ended in 1966 when a group of army officers killed most of the political leaders and took control of the country (a military coup). In 1967 the independence of the new state of Biafra was declared in the south east, starting the Nigerian civil war. Civilian rule was re-established in Nigeria in 1979. The end of the oil boom in the 1980s led to problems with paying teachers' wages and providing medicines for hospitals. In 1991 the World Bank found that Nigeria was the 13th poorest country in the world. Another military coup in 1994 led to a rule of fear across Nigeria.

Civilian rule was reintroduced in 1999, but Nigeria was left with many problems to overcome, including an economy in pieces, inefficient public services and weak infrastructure. The GNI was a third of what it had been in the 1980s and millions of people lived in slums, without access to basic facilities. Nigeria was seen by the world as corrupt and failing. More ethnic tensions flared between the Yoruba and Hausa groups and northern Nigeria was torn apart by religious disagreements between Muslim and Christian groups.

Elections in 2011 and 2015 were declared free and fair by international observers and Nigeria seems to have gained stable governance. More TNCs have developed businesses in Nigeria, including power plants owned by General Electric and IT developments through Microsoft, both from the USA. However, ethnic tensions still cause problems in Nigeria. Boko Haraem was founded in 2002 to oppose Western-style education in the north of Nigeria, but declared its intention to create an Islamic State in 2009, causing refugees to flee and many people to feel that the northern part of the country was unsafe.

Nigerian culture also varies according to its different groups. Nigerian cinema is known as 'Nollywood' and is the second largest film industry in the world (in terms of number of films made), behind India, but ahead of the USA.

Nigeria's changing industrial structure

The balance between different sectors of the economy

Nigeria's economy was originally dominated by **primary products**, including palm oil and crude oil. **Secondary industries** involved in manufacturing and processing developed under the British Empire and following independence, but growth slowed in the 1980s due to political problems.

The growth of manufacturing industry and the service sector

The discovery of oil in Nigeria fuelled economic growth and enabled huge investment into manufacturing. Now foreign investment is providing a new boost to secondary industries in Nigeria and also developing **tertiary industries** which provide a service, such as finance and retail. Nigeria was linked with Mexico, Turkey and Indonesia as **MINT countries** in 2011. The economies of these countries were predicted to grow rapidly and so they were seen as good places to invest in.

'Nigeria's reserves of oil have boosted the economy'

The role of transnational corporations (TNCs) in Nigeria

Shell Oil (Anglo-Dutch TNC) has been involved in the Niger Delta since the 1930s, investing huge amounts of money in extracting oil in very difficult conditions. Since setting up there, Shell has brought many advantages and disadvantages to Nigeria.

Benefits of Shell Oil in the Niger Delta:

- Pay taxes and increase export revenue
- Employ 65,000 Nigerians directly and another 250,000 indirectly
- Create a multiplier effect by giving contracts to Nigerian companies

Disadvantages of Shell Oil in the Niger Delta:

- Oil spills cause pollution of water and soil, causing problems for farming and fishing
- Gas flares pollute the air
- Security issues related to oil theft and disruption of supplies by military groups

Nigeria's changing political and trading relationships with the wider world

Nigeria's **trade relationships** have changed from trade with Britain and Portugal before colonisation, to close links with Britain as part of the Empire. Now Nigeria's main trade partners are Brazil, China, India, Japan, the US and the European Union. Nigeria also plays an important role in the Economic Community of West African States (ECOWAS), a trade bloc of 15 countries encouraging economic cooperation in the region.

These changing trade relationships reflect the change in **political relationships** as Nigeria became a British colony and then an independent nation and a regional leader in West Africa. Nigeria is still linked to Britain through the **Commonwealth**.

International aid in Nigeria

What type of aid does Nigeria receive?

- **Short term/emergency aid** – eg. Food and water in times of famine
- **Long term/developmental** – eg. Programmes to develop infrastructure, education, healthcare
- **Bilateral** – from one country to Nigeria
- **Multilateral** – from an organisation such as the World Bank
- **Non-governmental organisations (NGOs)** – eg. The Red Cross, Oxfam, etc

How does aid benefit Nigeria?

In 2014, the World Bank launched a $500million project for Nigeria, funding development projects & providing long term loans to businesses, helping to diversify the economy so it isn't so dependent on oil.

WaterAid is an example of an NGO working in Nigeria. Only three in ten people in Nigeria have access to a satisfactory toilet, so WaterAid is working with the Nigerian government to improve access to sanitation systems, and therefore reduce the risk of disease.

A typical toilet in rural Nigeria'

How has economic development affected Nigeria?

The impact of economic development on the environment

As Nigeria has developed economically and become a NEE it has had an impact on the environment.

Examples of positive impacts:

- Seven national parks protect valuable landscapes and habitats in Nigeria
- Nigeria is a member of the United Nations and so is working towards the **Sustainable Development Goals** (SDGs)

Examples of negatives:

- **Deforestation** means Nigeria has lost 70-80% of its forests to farming (for cash crops), logging and development of infrastructure and industry
- Hydropower dams have contributed to **desertification** in the north
- The Niger Delta has suffered from oil spills and burning gas, polluting the land, water and air

The impact of economic development on quality of life

Nigeria's economic development has also affected quality of life for its population, but this varies according to the area and ethnic group.

Examples of positives:

- Nigeria's **HDI** improved from 0.467 in 2005 to 0.534 in 2018 and all four statistics to calculate this showed improvement
- Life expectancy increased by 8.4 years between 1990 and 2018
- Examples of negatives:
- Nigeria's HDI of 0.534 in 2018 saw it ranked 158 out of 189 countries and classified in the low human development category
- People move to **squatter settlements** in urban areas which suffer from overcrowding, a lack of access to basic services, and pollution

Question 1 | Match the terms with their definitions

A	**Exchanging goods with other people**
B	**People who come from one country but live in other countries around the world**
C	**When new aspects are added to an economy so it isn't as reliant on one aspect**
D	**Businesses which operate in different countries**

diaspora	trade	transnational corporations	diversification

Question 2 | Are these statements true or false?	
Nigeria is located in West Africa.	true
The capital city of Nigeria is Lagos.	false (Abuja)
The Berlin Conference of 1884 was a meeting of European and African leaders to decide the future of Africa for the benefit of all	false
British people were never involved in slavery in Nigeria and brought an end to the Portuguese slave trade in Lagos.	False
Nigeria became independent from Britain in 1960.	~~Fa~~ True (military rule)
Nigeria has been ruled by democratically elected governments since independence.	False
An independent state of Biafra was declared in 1967, triggering a two-year civil war.	true
Oil exploitation has brought many benefits for the people in the Niger Delta.	false
Elections in Nigeria in 2011 and 2015 were declared free and fair.	true
'Nollywood' is the second largest film industry in the world, after Hollywood.	true
Nigeria is one of the MINT countries, along with Mexico, Indonesia and Turkey.	true
Nigeria is part of the Commonwealth	true
Nigeria is now a NEE and so doesn't receive aid.	False
Economic development has made more money available for environmental projects in Nigeria.	true
Farming for cash crops is helping Nigeria tackle deforestation.	False
Nigeria's HDI improved from 0.467 in 2005 to 0.534 in 2018.	true
Nigeria's employment structure shows a change over time, away from the primary sector and to the tertiary sector.	true

Question 3 | How have the following affected the development of Nigeria?

The country's boundaries being drawn without consideration of existing ethnic groups	
Having access to a sea port in Lagos	
Having extensive oil reserves	
Unstable government following independence	
Being a former colony of Britain	
Investment from TNCs	

Question 4 | Sort the statements to complete the table showing the benefits and disadvantages of Shell Oil in the Niger Delta.

- Pays taxes and increases export revenue
- Gas flares pollute the air
- Creates a multiplier effect by giving contracts to Nigerian companies
- Oil spills cause pollution of water and soil, causing problems for farming and fishing
- Employs 65,000 Nigerians directly and another 250,000 indirectly
- Security issues related to oil theft and disruption of supplies by military groups

Benefits of Shell Oil in the Niger Delta	Disadvantages of Shell Oil in the Niger Delta

Question 5 | Fill the gaps using the words below

Nigeria's ______________________________ have changed over time, from trade with Britain and Portugal before colonisation to close links with Britain as part of its Empire. Now Nigeria's main trade partners are Brazil, China, India, Japan, the US and the European Union. Nigeria also plays an important role in the Economic Community of West African States (ECOWAS), a trade bloc of 15 countries encouraging economic ____________________ in the region.

These changing trade relationships reflect the change in political relationships as Nigeria became a British ____________________ and then an independent nation and a regional leader in West Africa. Nigeria is still linked to Britain through the __________________________, a voluntary association of countries which were once part of the British Empire.

colony	commonwealth	trade relationships	cooperation

Question 6 | Complete the 'washing line of relative importance' to show how important political stability, natural resources and trade relationships are in the development of Nigeria's economy. Write a statement to support your choices.

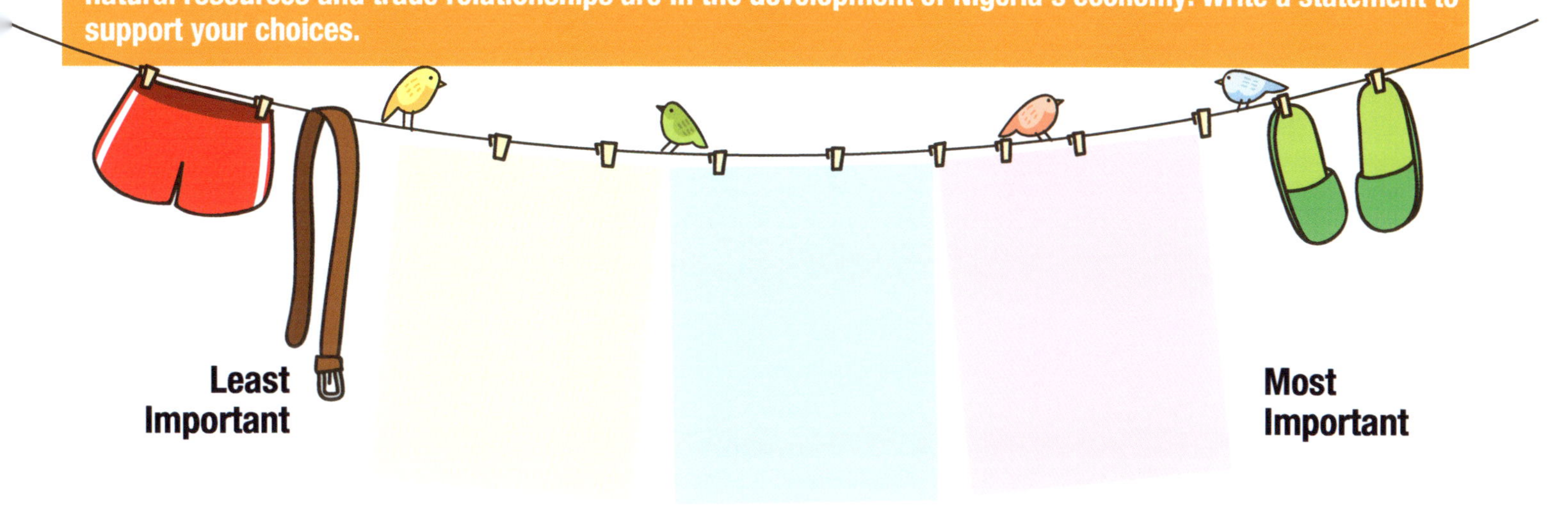

Question 7 | The economic development of Nigeria has improved the quality of life of its people'. Colour the thermometer to show how strongly you agree with this statement. Write a statement to support your choice. The best statements will refer to specific details related to Nigeria.

Strongly agree

Somewhat agree

Strongly disagree

Question 8 | Match the types of aid provided to Nigeria with the examples

Bilateral aid	From the World Bank
Multilateral aid	From Water Aid
Non-governmental organisation	From the UK government

Question 10 | Exam-style question.

Discuss how the changing political relationships of a LIC or NEE you have studied have affected its development. (6 marks)

KEY IDEA 4 MAJOR CHANGES IN THE ECONOMY OF THE UK HAVE AFFECTED, AND WILL CONTINUE TO AFFECT, EMPLOYMENT PATTERNS AND REGIONAL GROWTH

What you need to know: Economic futures in the UK
Causes of economic change: deindustrialisation and decline of traditional industrial base, globalisation and government policies
Moving towards a post-industrial economy: development of information technology, service industries, finance, research, science and business parks
Impacts of industry on the physical environment. An example of how modern industrial development can be more environmentally sustainable
Social and economic changes in the rural landscape in one area of population growth and one area of population decline
Improvements and new developments in road and rail infrastructure, port and airport capacity
The north–south divide. Strategies used in an attempt to resolve regional differences
The place of the UK in the wider world. Links through trade, culture, transport, and electronic communication. Economic and political links: the European Union (EU) and Commonwealth

This Study Book includes a summary of the UK case study. To see this case study in detail, scan the QR code below. You'll need to logged into your free mytutor2u account to access this resource.

INTRODUCTION

The UK economy was once dominated by primary industries involving exploiting raw materials, with most people living in the countryside. Since this time the UK has seen many changes in its economy, including the boom in manufacturing (secondary industries) following the Industrial Revolution, and the huge increase in tertiary industries since World War II, and the more recent growth in the quaternary sector (research and development).

Causes of economic change

Deindustrialisation and decline of traditional industrial base

Deindustrialisation (closure of **traditional industries**) struck parts of the UK a heavy blow. The closure of coalmines and steelworks went hand in hand with increased unemployment and poverty, particularly in northern areas of England, and southern parts of Wales.

The remains of Hatfield colliery, South Yorkshire

Globalisation

As countries such as Taiwan, Hong Kong, South Korea and Singapore (the four Asian tigers) began to produce manufactured goods and sell them around the world in the 1980s, UK industries found it difficult to compete with the lower labour costs. New machinery was used to boost productivity, but this meant fewer workers were needed so jobs were lost.

Globalisation was benefitting consumers but taking its toll on the UK's traditional industrial base. However, whilst some areas saw decline, the South East of England thrived, as the **tertiary and quaternary sectors** went from strength to strength.

Government policies

Industries had been developed as private businesses during and after the Industrial Revolution, but the UK found itself ready for further change following World War II. The Labour government grouped many industries together to create state-run organisations such as British Rail and the National Coal Board. This made it easier to rebuild and modernise industries after the war and was known as **nationalisation.**

The Conservative Government that gained power in 1979, was keen to **privatise** state-run industries by selling them to private shareholders. State industries which had been kept running using government money (subsidies) needed to become more efficient to survive and many closed, leading to further job losses.

Moving towards a post-industrial economy

Some people argue that the UK is now a **post-industrial society**. The economy has much less manufacturing industry now, and is dominated by the tertiary sector as well as seeing major growth in the quaternary sectors. Together the tertiary and quaternary sectors now employ over 80% of UK workers.

<table>
<tr><th>Sector</th><th>1991</th><th>2020</th></tr>
<tr><td>Primary</td><td>3%</td><td>1.00%</td></tr>
<tr><td>Secondary</td><td>28%</td><td>17.66%</td></tr>
<tr><td>Tertiary</td><td>54%</td><td rowspan="2">81.34%</td></tr>
<tr><td>Quaternary</td><td>15%</td></tr>
</table>

Development of information technology

IT has transformed how we live and work, and is one of the main reasons the UK has moved towards a post-industrial economy. Computers allow us to store and access huge amounts of data, and the internet has enabled instant communication between people right across the globe. Across the UK 1.3 million people are employed in IT.

Service industries, finance and research

Major developments in the UK economy include:

- Service industries account for over three-quarters of UK workers, in sectors such as tourism, retail, hospitality, education and healthcare – providing a wide variety of services.
- Finance is a big part of the service sector, including banking and insurance. The UK is an important global centre for finance. Financial services employ around 2 million workers across the UK, and accounts for 10% of **GDP (gross domestic product).**
- The UK research sector includes organisations such as universities, charities, pharmaceutical companies and the NHS. It employs around 60,000 people and contributes approximately £3 billion to the UK economy.

The Paintworks is home to Bristol's cultural quarter'

Science and business parks

Since the 1980s developments have appeared on the edge of settlements in the UK, making the most of the space and good road links available:

- **Science parks** – a site for a group of research and IT based businesses, usually linked to a university, so that they can share facilities and employ highly qualified graduates. Example: Cambridge Science Park, close to the University of Cambridge.
- **Business parks** – areas of land used by different businesses, usually in purpose-built buildings on the edge of towns. These parks have plenty of space as land is cheap, so can have large buildings and car parks and are usually easy to get to using motorways and A roads. Businesses on one site may work together. Example: Aztec West, next to the junction of the M4 and M5 motorways.

Impacts of industry on the physical environment

Primary sector

Mining and quarrying involve noise and dust and can cause vibrations in the local area, whilst test sites for fracking in the UK have seen minor earthquakes. Waste materials may be piled up in heaps, affecting the visual landscape.

BUT the Environment Agency in the UK monitors these industries and can fine private businesses if pollutants are released illegally.

Secondary sector

Factories may release pollution into the air or water and waste from production may be sent to landfill sites. Factories are often large and so may look unattractive.

BUT locating factories on business parks means they are away from residential areas, reducing their visual and noise impact.

Tertiary sector

Shops usually encourage people to buy as much as they can, leading to a boom in consumption, which some see as a wasteful way to use natural resources. Shops also produce waste, and people living near big shops may find them ugly and noisy.

BUT many supermarkets have limited their deals so that customers aren't encouraged to over buy (i.e. BOGOF) and are improving their rates of recycling.

Paintworks in Bristol: An example of how modern industrial development can be more environmentally sustainable

Phoenix Wharf, to the east of Bristol city centre, was once home to a paint and varnish factory. Verve took over in 2004 and turned the site into a mixed-use development, including space for new industry.

The Paintworks is home to Bristol's cultural quarter'

Today, this site known as Paintworks is sustainable because:

- This brownfield development has brought a city centre location back to life, reducing the pressure for housing on the rural/urban fringe
- The site has a green travel plan; and secure cycle spaces are provided
- If people live and work in the same area they won't need to commute, reducing traffic congestion and emissions
- The Ethical Property Company has set up Streamline, an affordable workspace which can be shared by up to 20 organisations.

The site is part of a district heat network, an organisation which aims to cut emissions.

Changing rural landscapes

It isn't only urban areas which have changed in the UK because of the changing structure of local economies. Rural landscapes in the UK have also experienced social and economic changes, but the impacts vary depending on whether these rural areas are facing population decline or population growth.

Outer Hebrides is a group of islands off the west coast of Scotland which have experienced **depopulation** as people have moved away. 46,000 people lived on the islands in 1901, but this had dropped to below 27,000 by 2018.

- **Social impacts** – schools close when there aren't enough students to keep them going. When working age people move away it creates an ageing population, with fewer people to do the work, and fewer people to look after the elderly.
- **Economic impacts** – businesses such as post offices shut when they don't have enough customers.

The Outer Hebrides has experienced major population decline'

South Cambridgeshire is a rural area which has experienced **population growth**. In 2009 its population was 143 600, but by 2018 the population had increased to 156 000 and further growth was expected

- Social impacts – villages have grown, meaning more house building, traffic and noise. This changes the nature of the villages, which once had close communities. Young people move out of the area to find affordable housing.
- Economic impacts – house prices rise (due to demand) and pressure grows on services. Original residents may welcome the boost of new people coming to the area and people with businesses may appreciate new customers.

South Cambridgeshire is an example of **suburbanisation** of the countryside.

Improving infrastructure across the UK

Infrastructure is the physical and organisational structures that allow the UK to function. This includes services and facilities such as roads and railways, water supply, electricity network, telecommunications, etc. Transport infrastructure is vital to the UK economy.

Current infrastructure improvements in the UK include:

- **Road** – 2014 road investment strategy - £15 billion – aims to improve capacity and condition of roads
- **Rail** – projects include High Speed 2* (HS2) and London's Crossrail
- **Ports** – the largest ports are owned by private businesses which are investing in improved infrastructure e.g. Liverpool 2 deep container port
- **Airports** – in 2015 a government report recommended building a third runway at Heathrow (just west of London, and Europe's biggest and busiest airport). However a decision has yet to be made as it is a controversial proposal and many fear it will increase CO_2 emissions further.

High Speed 2 (HS2)

The High Speed 2 (HS2) project will connect London with Birmingham and onwards to Sheffield, Leeds and Manchester. In 2020 work began on this major rail investment project, however there is still debate about its benefits.

Arguments for HS2:

- Travel times will be reduced and areas in the midlands and north of England will become more attractive to industry, leading to investment
- Increased rail capacity will encourage people to use public transport, helping the government towards meeting environmental targets
- 50,000 jobs will be created by the scheme
- HS2 is expected to create 2000 apprenticeships.

Arguments against HS2:

- Hundreds of wild sites are threatened by HS2, including ancient woodlands, lakes and meadows
- 1,740 buildings (including homes) will be demolished
- The Stop HS2 group argue that there is no business case for HS2, no environmental case and no money to pay for it
- The cost of the scheme is huge. HS2 was originally costed at £56 billion in 2015 but in 2020 government ministers admitted it was running £30 billion over budget, and could cost as much as £98 billion

Many are concerned over the environmental impact of HS2

The north–south divide

Some suggest that there are differences between the north and south of the UK in terms of culture and economy, with employment rates, house prices, poverty rates and even health showing distinct differences in people's lives in the north and south of the country. One reason for these differences is that the north was hit particularly hard by deindustrialisation, whereas the south has always had a strong tertiary sector.

Strategies to tackle the north-south divide:

- **Northern Powerhouse** – Government strategy launched in 2015 to develop the economies of the major cities in northern England
- **Local enterprise partnerships (LEPs)** – Voluntary partnerships between local authorities and private businesses aiming to encourage investment in the area
- **Enterprise Zones** – Zones designated for support by the government to attract new businesses to an area – 24 have been set up since 2011.

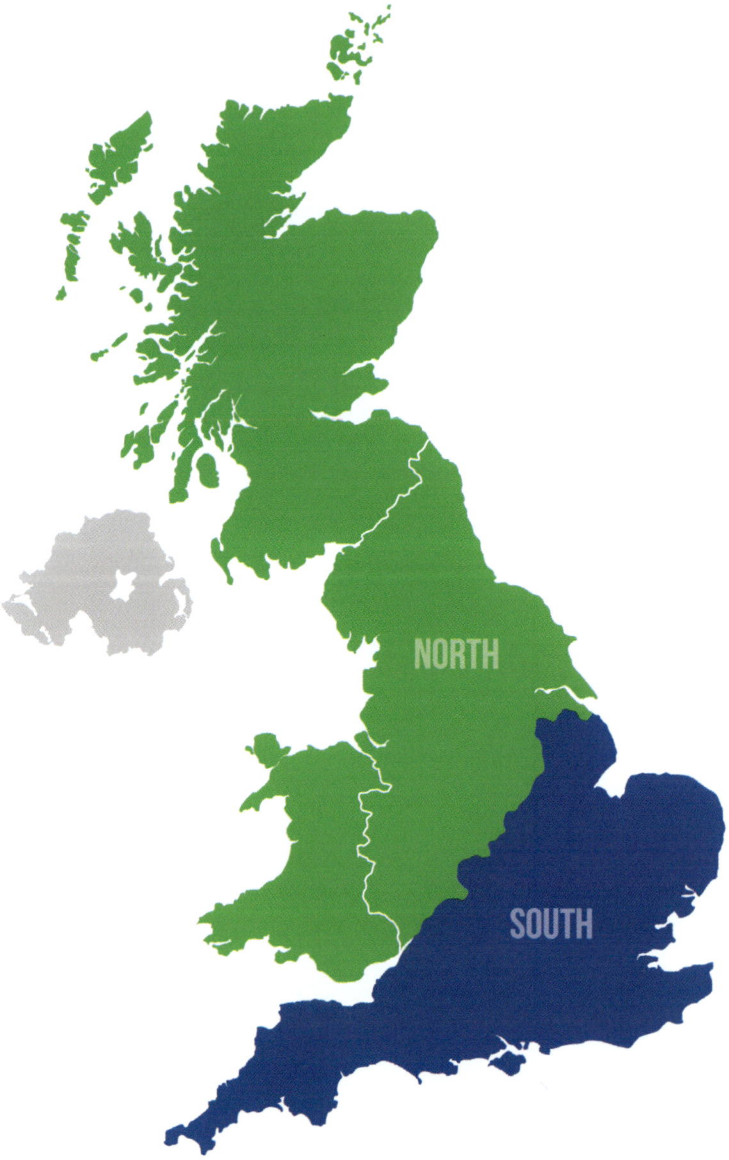

The place of the UK in the wider world

The UK is part of a **globalised world,** linked in many ways. These links are dynamic – they have changed over time and will continue to change in the future.

- **Trade** – exchange of goods and services using the internet, roads, rail and air transport
- **Culture** – the way of life of a society, including music, fashion, writing, painting and more. Films and TV programmes play an important role in spreading cultures around the world
- **Transport** – Whilst the UK is somewhat isolated as an island, it is still linked to the wider world through the Channel Tunnel, ports and airports
- **Electronic communication** – The UK is connected to the wider world through internet connections, most of which use submarine high power cables.

The UK's economic and political links have changed over time.

The Commonwealth – exploration and empire

In 1580 Sir Francis Drake completed his circumnavigation of the world, one of many British explorers who set out on ships to discover the world in this era. Once links had been made with a place, **trade** could begin. Between 1763 and 1783 Britain had a large **empire**, including colonies in America and the West Indies, but this ended with the American Revolution. Between 1783 and 1924 the second British Empire was mainly made up of India and African colonies. Ships began to transport convicts from England to Australia in 1788. The Irish Act of Union united Britain and Ireland in 1801.

In 1914 Britain declared war on Germany in response to the invasion of Belgium. After 1924 Britain began to let go of the Empire as it was too expensive, difficult to protect and many areas didn't want to be ruled by Britain.

In 1926 the Balfour Declaration created the **British Commonwealth of Nations,** with Canada, Australia, New Zealand and South Africa as members. The Commonwealth Secretariat was set up in 1965.

The European Union

In 1939 Britain entered into World War II, then at the end of the war in 1945 Britain became a founding member of the **United Nations**. The idea that countries could cooperate together to strengthen their economies led to the establishment of the European Economic Community (EEC).

The UK became a member of the EEC in 1973, becoming part of a free trade community. The EEC became the **European Union** in 1993. In the same year the UK Independence Party (UKIP) was formed. The UK government held a Brexit referendum to find out if voters wanted to leave or remain in the EU in 2016. The result of the poll was 'leave' by a narrow margin, and the UK formally left the EU on 31st January 2020.

You will need to look at additional detail about this case study on the website (using the QR code at the start of this topic) to answer some of these questions.

Question 1 | Match the terms with their definitions

A	A time after traditional industries when the tertiary and quaternary sectors are most important
B	The decline of traditional industries
C	The network of power, transport and facilities needed for the country to function
D	The world becoming increasingly connected

post-industrial society	infrastructure	deindustrialisation	globalisation

Question 2 | Are these statements true or false?	
Primary industries exploit raw materials e.g. farming, mining	
Secondary industries provide a service e.g. a shop	
Tertiary industries make things e.g. a car factory	
Quaternary industries involve research and high technology industries	
The Industrial Revolution meant that factories were set up where people lived, and raw materials were transported to them	
Deindustrialisation only affected the north of England	
Deindustrialisation led to an increase in unemployment	
Globalisation benefitted the South East of England as tertiary and quaternary industries boomed	
Nationalisation involves grouping private businesses together and the government taking control	
Once a business is nationalised it can't be privatised again	
Business Parks are areas of land used by different businesses, with other organisations such as hotels and gyms	
Science Parks are the same thing as Business Parks	
Mining and quarrying can be noisy and dusty, damaging the physical environment	
The Environment Agency monitors industries and issues fines if they release pollutants illegally	
Secondary industries don't harm the physical environment	
The Outer Hebrides has suffered depopulation and has an ageing population	
South Cambridgeshire is an urban area which is growing rapidly	
Liverpool2 is a new container port being built to double the capacity of the Port of Liverpool	
Everyone agrees that HS2 will be of benefit to the UK	
The Northern Powerhouse strategy aims to develop the economies of northern cities and tackle the north-south divide	
The UK is linked to the wider world through trade, culture, transport and electronic communication	
The British Empire used to include colonies in North America	
Countries which used to be in the British Empire have to be part of the Commonwealth	
Britain was a founding member of the United Nations	
Britain was a founding member of the European Union	

Question 4 | Look at the table below, showing the employment structure of the UK in 1991 and 2017. What conclusions can you draw about changes in the UK economy using this data?

<table>
<tr><th>Sector</th><th>1991</th><th>2017</th></tr>
<tr><td>Primary</td><td>3%</td><td>1.00%</td></tr>
<tr><td>Secondary</td><td>28%</td><td>17.66%</td></tr>
<tr><td>Tertiary</td><td>54%</td><td rowspan="2">81.34%</td></tr>
<tr><td>Quaternary</td><td>15%</td></tr>
</table>

Question 4 | How have the following affected the UK economy?

Deindustrialisation

Government policies

Globalisation

Question 5 | Sort the statements to complete the Venn diagram to show characteristics of science parks and business parks.

1 Built on edge of towns or cities where there is cheaper land and plenty of space
2 Usually have links to universities
3 Located near to motorway junctions and airports
4 Organisations may benefit from working together
5 May include organisations such as hotels, gyms, coffee shops etc.
6 The first one in the UK was located in Cambridge
7 Need to offer excellent conditions to attract the top graduates to work there

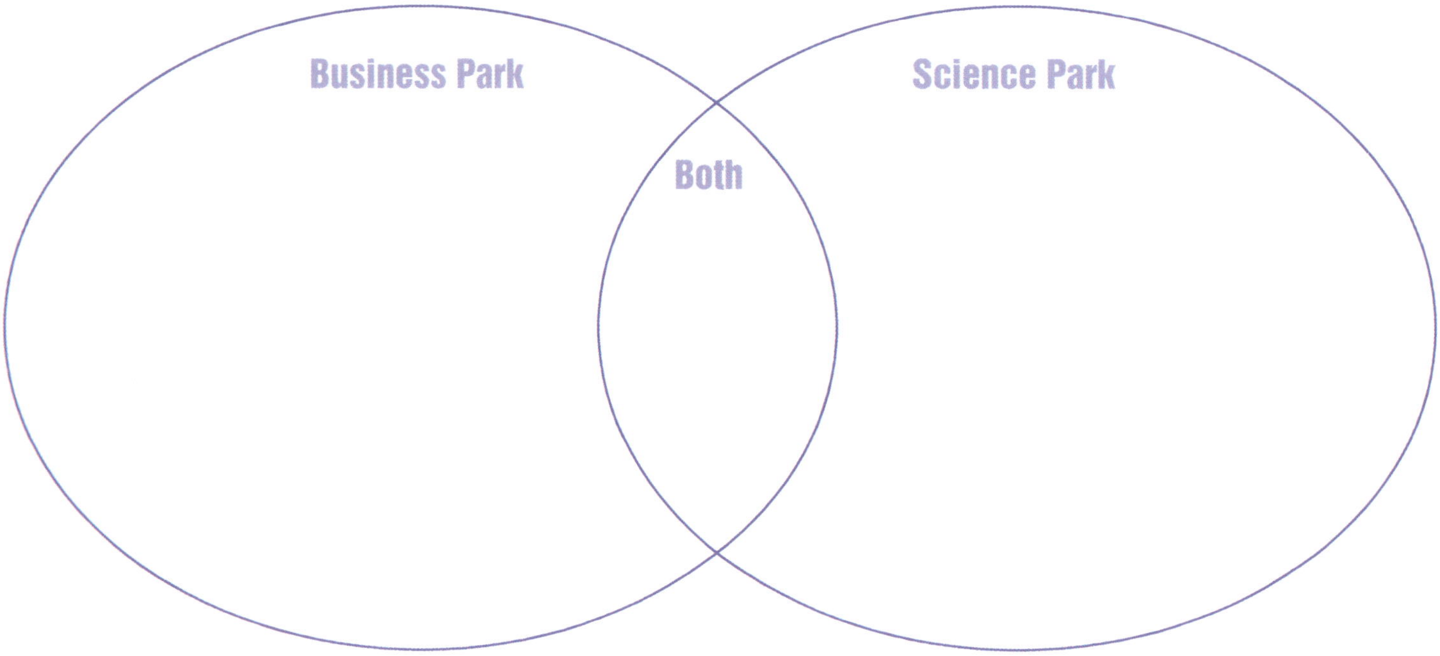

Question 6 | Look at the information in the table below and answer the questions.

Brighton - City in South East England

- Life expectancy of women 82.5yrs
- Life expectancy of men 77.1yrs
- Average house price £396 369
- Unemployment rate 6%
- 5+ GCSEs (inc. Eng & Maths) 55.4%
- Average salary £25 563

Glasgow - City in the west of Scotland

- Life expectancy of women 78.9yrs
- Life expectancy of men 73.1yrs
- Average house price £186 705
- Unemployment rate 5.9%
- 5+ GCSEs (inc. Eng & Maths) N/A
- Average salary £26 289

Bristol - City in South West of England

- Life expectancy of women 81.9yrs
- Life expectancy of men 77.2 yrs
- Average house price £333,686
- Unemployment rate 3.8%
- 5+ GCSEs (inc Eng & Maths) 51%
- Average salary £28 203

Bradford - City in northern England

- Life expectancy of women 80.4yrs
- Life expectancy of men 76.4yrs
- Average house price £135,798
- Unemployment rate 5.1%
- 5+ GCSEs (inc Eng & Maths) 52%
- Average salary £21 058

What evidence is there in this table that the north-south divide exists?

What evidence is there that the north-south divide doesn't exist?

Overall, do you think the information in this table shows that the north-south divide exists? Justify your answer?

Question 7 | Complete the 'washing line of relative importance' to show how important trade, culture and transport are in connecting the UK to a globalised world. Write a statement to support your choices.

Question 8 | The Commonwealth plays a significant role in the UK's economic and political links'. Colour the thermometer to show how strongly you agree with this statement. Write a statement to support your choice. The best statements will refer to specific details related to the Commonwealth.

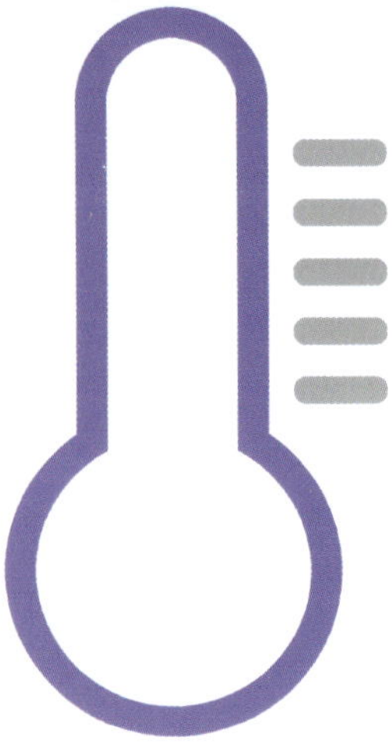

Strongly agree	
Somewhat agree	
Strongly disagree	

Question 9 | Sort the following statements into the table, to show the social and economic impacts of population change on two rural areas.

- Businesses such as post offices shut when they don't have enough customers.
- Schools close when there aren't enough students to keep them going.
- House prices rise and pressure grows on services.
- Original residents may welcome the boost of new people coming to the area and people with businesses may appreciate new customers.
- When working age people move away it creates an ageing population, with fewer people to do the work and care for the elderly.
- Young people move out of the area to find affordable housing.
- Villages have grown, meaning more house building, traffic and noise. This changes the nature of the villages, which once had close communities

	Social impacts	Economic impacts
Outer Hebrides rural population decline		

South Cambridgeshire rural population growth		

Question 10 | Exam-style question.

Evaluate the impact of improvements or new developments in transport infrastructure on the economy of the UK. (9 marks)

GLOSSARY

Key term	Definition
Access to safe water	The percentage of people who are able to get hold of water which is safe to drink (won't make them ill)
Ageing population	Population with a high median age; the proportion of the population aged 65 years and over is high
Bilateral aid	Aid from the government of one country to another
Birth rate	The number of births per thousand people per year
Business park	An area providing units for businesses and associated facilities such as hotels, gyms and coffee shops; often found on the edge of cities
Classification	A way of dividing something up into categories
Colonialism	Control by one country over another country and its people
Colony	A country which is governed by another country and which is occupied by people from that country
Commonwealth	Voluntary organisation of countries which used to be part of the British Empire and who support each other in promoting democracy, peace and cooperation
Conflict	Can range from a disagreement between people to large scale protests and wars
Consequences	The result or effect of something
Continuum	A sequence which ranks items according to a particular factor. One way of looking at development across the world
Corruption	dishonest or fraudulent behaviour by those in power in a country
Cultural change	When people's lifestyles change, often as a result of outside influences
Debt crisis	Occurs when a country has borrowed money that it is then unable to repay
Debt relief	Letting countries off some of their debts if they meet certain conditions
Deforestation	The cutting down of trees, often on a large scale
Deindustrialisation	The decline of traditional industries such as the coal mining and steel industries
Demographic transition model	Diagram showing how population changes over time as a country develops
Desertification	The process by which once productive land becomes too dry and lacking in nutrients to sustain plant growth
Development	A change which leads to improvement
Development gap	The gap in development between the richest and the poorest countries
Diaspora	The spread of people from their original homeland or country
Disparity	A great difference in a certain factor such as wealth, across an area of a country
Diversify	To become more varied
Economic change	When the way money is earnt and spent changes, or the jobs that people do changes
Economic measures	Focus on money, jobs and the economy
Economy	Production and consumption of goods and services and the supply of money
Electronic communication	Transfer of data from one place to another eg. by e-mail
Employment structure	How the workforce is divided between the primary, secondary, tertiary and quaternary sectors
Environmental impact	A change that affects the natural landscape and its habitats
Environmentally sustainable	Meeting the needs of the present without damaging people or the environment for the future
European Union	An organisation of European countries to reduce trade barriers and increase cooperation between member countries.
Fairtrade	An organisation which uses a logo to show that producers have been paid a fairer price for their goods and a community premium has been collected
Finance	Management of money
Food and water insecurity	When people do not have access to sufficient and safe food or water supplies
Formal economy	Work in which people are employed, receiving regular wages and benefits such as sick pay; businesses that pay tax to the government
Globalisation	Ways in which the world is becoming increasingly connected
Government policies	Decisions made by the government about how to manage something

Key term	Definition
Gross national income (GNI) per capita	A measure of a country's wealth that takes the income of the whole country and divides it by the number of people in the country. This includes the value of goods and services produced.
High income country (HIC)	A country with an income per person of $12,695 or more (based on 2021 figures)
Historical causes	When something happens because of the way things were in the past
Human Development Index	A composite measure of development which takes into account wealth, health and education
Industrial development	The expansion of industries in an area, such as factories
Industrial structure	The percentage of people who work in each job sector ; also known as employment structure
Infant mortality rate	The number of children who die before their first birthday, per 1000 live births per year
Informal economy	Work done without the official knowledge of the government; businesses that don't pay taxes
Information technology	Systems such as computers that are used for storing, retrieving and sending information
Infrastructure	Basic structures such as roads, water and energy supplies, and waste disposal; the systems that are needed for a country to be able to function efficiently
Intermediate (or appropriate) technology	simple technology which can be easily used and maintained and is community-led
International aid	Aid from one country to another in the form of money, goods or services
International migration	When people move from one country to another
Investment	Using money for something in the hope of making a profit
Low income country (LIC)	A country with an income per person of $1,046 - $4,695 (based on 2021 figures)
Life expectancy	The average number of years a person is expected to live
Literacy rate	The percentage of people who can read and write (sometimes expressed as male and female separately to high light inequality in access to education)
Long term aid	Aid which is used for rebuilding and developing a place in order to improve quality of life, often over several years
Manufacturing industry	Part of the secondary sector, making goods
Megacity	A city with a population of more than 10 million people
Microfinance loans	Loans given to people who can't access normal banks. They are able to borrow small amounts of money to invest in projects to improve their quality of life.
Multilateral aid	Aid from multiple donors organised through an organisation such as the World Bank, and given to individual countries
Multiplier effect	When one event leads to another, eg. a factory closing down leads to job losses, which lead to less money being spent in the local economy, etc
Nationalisation	The transfer of key industries from private to state ownership by the government
Natural increase	When the birth rate of a country is greater than the death rate, leading to population growth
Newly emerging economies (NEEs)	Countries which used to rely on agriculture but have recently seen growth in their industries and increased income and development
Non-governmental organisation (NGO)	A charity or pressure group that raises awareness of issues and organises the distribution of aid/setting up up of aid projects
North - South divide	A theory that there is a division between the north and south of England in terms of the economy and culture
People per doctor	The number of people in a place divided by the number of doctors who are available to treat them
Physical causes	When something happens because of natural processes
Physical environmen	The natural landscape and habitat of a place
Political relationships	How leaders and countries interact with one another
Population pyramids	These show the population structure of a place in terms of age and sex (also known as age-sex pyramids)
Port and airport capacity	The amount of people or freight (goods) which can be handled at a port or airport
Post-industrial economy	When traditional industry has declined, and tertiary and quaternary industries dominate the economy
Primary products	Raw materials extracted from the land or the sea such as coal, wood and fish
Primary sector	Exploiting natural resources to gain raw materials eg.farming, fishing, forestry, mining, quarrying
Privatisation	The transfer of key industries from public to private ownership
Quality of life	How good a person's life is based on how healthy they are, whether or not they've had a good education, etc
Quaternary sector	Research, development and high technology industries

Key term	Definition
Refugee	A person who has been forced to leave their country because of war, persecution or a natural disaster
Regional differences	How one part of a country is different from another
Road and rail infrastructure	The buildings and equipment needed to have a road and rail network
Rural landscape	Somewhere in the countryside (not built-up)
Science park	A concentration of research and high technology businesses with close links to a university
Secondary sector/industry	Making something or putting components together eg. a car factory
Short term aid	Keeps people alive in the short term and minimises the death toll, often after a natural disaster (also known as emergency aid)
Social change	When the way a society is organised or its structure changes
Social measures	Focus on people's living standards and quality of life
Squatter settlements	Areas of housing built on land that doesn't belong to the people living there (can be seen as a problematic term as often people do pay rent – informal settlement is a good alternative)
Stimulating the economy	Measures to get the economy to become more productive
Suburbanisation	The outward growth of towns and cities, which may swallow up villages on the outskirts of the urban area
Sustainable/ sustainability	Actions which meet the needs of the present generation without reducing the ability of future generations to meet their needs
Tertiary sector	Service industries e,g. retail, banking, teaching
Tourism	Holidays and visits to places of interest, and the industry that support this
Trade	The exchange of goods or services
Trade blocs	Groups of countries who work together to trade without barriers
Trading relationships	Agreements for exchanging goods between different places
Traditional industries	Industries which were first established in a place eg. coal mines and steel making in the UK
Transnational corporations (TNCs)	Business organisations based in more than one country
Uneven development	When some places are more developed than others
Urbanisation	Increase in the proportion of people living in urban areas (towns and cities)
Wealth	How much money or how many possessions someone has
World Bank	Global bank with 189 member countries
Youthful population	Population with a low median age; the proportion of the population aged 15 years and under is high

NOTES

Please scan the above QR Code to access the suggested answers for this book.

www.tutor2u.net/geography

AQA | GCSE | Geography

SKU: 05-4130-30429-03 | ISBN: 978-1915610171